Giving Meaning to Life in the Face of Losses

HEALING THE EMOTIONAL AND PHYSICAL PAIN LEFT BY GRIEF

Araceli García

All rights reserved. No part of this work may be reproduced, stored in a retrieval system, or transmitted in any form or by any means (electronic, mechanical, photocopying, recording, or otherwise) without prior written permission from the copyright holders, except for brief quotations with proper source acknowledgment. Infringement of these rights may constitute a violation of intellectual property law.

The content of this work is the responsibility of the author and does not necessarily reflect the opinions of the publishing house. All texts and images were provided by the author, who is solely responsible for their rights.

Published by Ibukku, LLC
www.ibukku.com
Cover design: Ángel Flores Guerra Bistrain
Design and layout: Diana Patricia González Juárez
Copyright © 2024 Araceli García
ISBN Paperback: 978-1-68574-980-4
ISBN Hardcover: 978-1-68574-982-8
ISBN eBook: 978-1-68574-981-1

Table of Content

Chapter 1
Personality in the Face of Grief and Loss   15

Chapter 2
Grief   19

Chapter 3
The Enigma of Death   31
    The Child in the Face of Death   33
    The Adolescent in the Face of Death   35
    The Adult in the Face of Death   36
    Old Age in the Face of Death   37

Chapter 4
Pain   39
    Pain Variants   40
    Classification of pain   43
    How to deal with pain?   44
    Is there pain in natural death?   44
    Factors that cause pain   45
    Physiological Factors   46
    Emotional Factors   46
    Symptoms   48

Chapter 5
Loss   51
    Starting from What is Lost   51
    What Do I Lose When I Lose?   52
    Expressing Emotions and Feelings   56
    Missing   58
    Attachment   59

Chapter 6
Promoting Autonomy   61
    Stress Reduction   61
    Distress and Anxiety   63
    Depression   68
    Improving Quality of Life   72

Adaptive Process	73
Test to Understand Your Attitude Toward Grief or Loss	77
Dynamic	78
Supportive Exercises	78
Techniques	79
Tips	82

I dedicate this book...

An experience of continuing to live despite the losses and the pain left by the absence of what I no longer have, yet I am left with the memory of what was lived.

Grief is a great teacher that teaches us to fight to reclaim life, in the face of that feeling of not being able to stand and feeling that bitter loneliness and great emptiness.

It seems impossible that only absence and memories of what was shared remains. With love, I give thanks, accept my reality, and say goodbye.

And when I transcend from this plane, I hold my hopes that we will meet again along the way. In the meantime, I choose to give meaning to life despite what has been lost.

ACKNOWLEDGMENTS

To my son Edwin, primarily for being the source of inspiration for this project, even though he has transcended this material plane.

To my family for being a fundamental source of motivation in my life.

To my friends for encouraging every step I take in life.

To the people who, with their trust, inspire me to be better.

To love and respect that I feel every day.

PROLOGUE

The purpose of this reading is to provide a better perspective on identifying how emotional and physical pain relate to grief or loss.

It is essential to recognize that human beings are born with a potential they can develop throughout their lives. However, this potential may vary from one individual to another, depending on each person's ability and resolution to ensure that the process of coping with loss is satisfactory.

In the field of mental health, this direct way of thinking has led to the emergence of simplistic explanations regarding the causes of behavior and the reasons for illness. The mind bears the paradoxical responsibility of controlling the body, creating a conflict between the two, which is reflected in physical illnesses, emotional conflicts, relationship failures, and intellectual incapacity. From this perspective, the symptom can be considered an effort by the person to adapt and survive, as they perceive themselves as residents of a strange, hostile, and toxic system.

When facing a loss, psychophysical, biopsychosocial, consoling or containing past experiences are revived, leading to a sensation of emptiness due to the absence.

Thus, the grieving process is linked to emotions, mental representations, sensations, and behaviors associated with affective loss, frustration, or pain.

The integration of a person (their emotions, thoughts, and behaviors) requires staying in touch with their life force and being willing to take risks. The will and ability to gain new awareness in the process of learning and change, both cognitively and emotionally, is necessary, even though memory sometimes falters when recalling emotional lessons and the notion of survival in the face of loss.

Within the uncertainties, we can find strategies that help the individual or the family discover their own answers, serving as an aid to the person, a representation that allows them to be located within themselves.

On the other hand, when discussing cultures and religions based on a model of threat and reward, it is considered that the dependence on these principles leads to a "suitable" lifestyle and promotes good mental health. It is important to give oneself the opportunity to grow in the context of improving life and to prepare for losses, including death, but with a sense of emotional balance, mental clarity, and spiritual peace.

An individual task is to identify the resources to confront loss; it is crucial to find alternatives and be able to diminish emotions, feelings of anguish, and stress. In this way, one can seek the physical well-being of the person, achieving relief from symptoms without trying to prolong survival, suffering, hope, or agony in the face of any loss. This will also help improve thoughts and quality of life, contributing to preparation for death, losses, or attachments with emotional balance and mental peace.

Thoughts and words are a form of vital energy that has the capacity (and has been sustainably demonstrated) to interact with the organism and produce very profound physical changes.

In studies such as Neuroimmunology, we learn mind-body connection keys, explaining why the mind and emotions affect the health of our body.

Meanwhile, Psychoneuroimmunobiology shows us the link that exists between thought, words, mindset, and human physiology. A connection that challenges the traditional paradigm.

INTRODUCTION

It is possible to find answers in the relationship that the individual perceives in physical and emotional pain in the face of losses and grief.

The importance of identifying the issues of physical and emotional pain is to find a balance and regulate emotions that affect daily life, thereby discovering one's own resources to manage pain.

There are factors that intervene in pain, such as stress due to the physical and mental reactions of the individual in adapting to changes.

When discussing stress, one can identify the body's response to external conditions that disturb the emotional harmony of the person, thus paving the way for emotional and physical pain. In this reaction, almost all organs and functions of the body are involved, including the brain, nerves, heart, blood flow, hormonal levels, digestion, and muscular function, so that the body becomes unbalanced due to the various functions that accelerate unnecessarily.

The book invites readers to identify and evaluate the most common painful manifestations that arise in response to any type of loss.

When we talk about pain, it is worth mentioning that it is a localized and subjective sensory perception that can be more or less intense, bothersome, or unpleasant, and that is felt in a specific part of the body; it is the result of excitation or stimulation of specialized sensory nerve endings.

However, there is another kind of pain involved in situations of loss and grief, such as intense feelings of sorrow, suffering, frustration, sadness, pity, depression, anguish, among others, which are considered emotional or psychological in nature.

In this way, it is important to identify one's own resources to control stress, tension, or harshness in the face of a diagnosis or painful event that may imply more suffering than necessary. Resistance is another factor that can manifest to produce pain and increase the difficulty of enduring, tolerating, or suffering unnecessarily at times.

In the face of unpleasant news, such as a diagnosis, a significant loss like a job, marriage, something material, or any relational bond, including death, tension begins to subject the body not only physically but also between reason and feeling. The physiological consequence will be a desire to flee from the scenario that provokes or confronts one violently.

This highlights the great importance of knowing the resources that one has individually for direct confrontation, as the psyche and body are physically affected by the disorganization of thoughts and ideas in the face of the separation from what was lost, allowing for a modification of an uncomfortable situation and the ability to lessen pain.

Considering grief as a process in response to the absence of something significant is to face a challenge of being able to implant life concepts, re-signify, and give another meaning to existence, reducing physical and psychological suffering, while also achieving well-being to live and die with dignity.

On the other hand, pillars such as attachment and individual resources regarding the concepts of loss, death, life, and absence, far from being enemies in a grieving process, can be collaborators in facing pain, suffering, the stress of separation, depression, despair, anger, fear…

Neimeyer discusses grief as a process of meaning restoration, indicating that the way one reacts to the loss will depend on the intimacy of what has been lost and how resources for adaptation are found. Factors that can exacerbate pain include guilt, anxiety, and the role of attachment, which can lead to emotional and physical illness, depending on the nature of the relationship maintained with the individual or object, potentially triggering a heart attack or stroke, as illustrated in his book *Learning from Loss*.

Some psychiatric disorders are expressions of pathological grief, and these disorders often include states of anxiety, depression, and even more than one type of personality disorder.

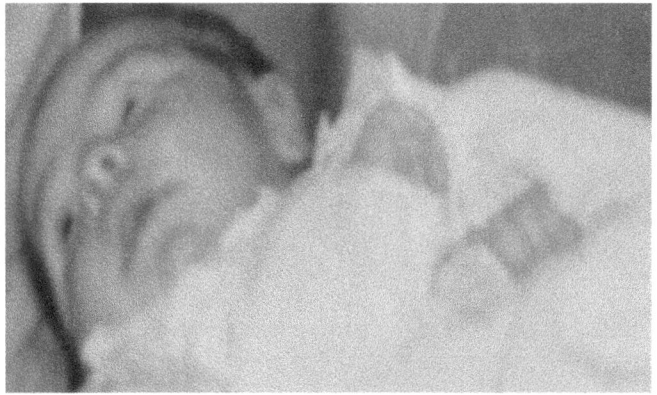

It is not possible to experience the joy of birth without suffering the pain of the farewell to the umbilical cord that provides security!

Chapter 1
Personality in the Face of Grief and Loss

And suddenly... What just happened?!... A GREAT SILENCE, I only feel unknown sensations s if my body is warning me of danger; how should I react to what's being done to me? I open my eyes and see different colors, there are unfamiliar smells, why are they touching me? I start to feel a great emptiness, they're cutting off what gave me security, what fed me, that feeling of tranquility, peace, and well-being is being taken away. That emptiness is hard to describe, it's something that hurts not just physically, it hurts that they're taking something "mine" from me. How strange it feels, there are people, but I feel alone against everything outside. My umbilical cord, give it back! I don't want to feel all this!

How do I stop feeling this unpleasant sensation that's possibly called "pain"? Yes, my soul hurts, my body hurts, it hurts to lose what I had, and now what's next? Is it fear, sadness? I no longer know if I feel discomfort or if I'm angry. I just lost what has been with me throughout my growth, I lost that trust and joy I once had... "I just lost everything."

Personality in the Face of Loss and Death

Personality begins at birth and is lost with death, according to Article 22 of the Federal Civil Code.

In some cases, we can talk about a scheduled birth date, but we don't know the date of death. There's a mystery wrapped around the word "death," as we don't know how to deal with it, nor do we know what to feel or how to process it. However, within the same mystery that death holds, we also find the fears of how to transcend and what pain there will be. Though some authors suggest that death itself doesn't hurt, what hurts is feeling the process and what death represents for each person.

From birth, we are already exposed to creating emotional relationships, learning to endure and tolerate discomfort, annoyance, and pain, whether it be physical, emotional, or the need to resist suffering. It's worth mentioning that the right hemisphere of the brain acts as a regulator of psychobiological states (including emotional states) and provides the neurobiological foundation for the experience of communicating with others. Meanwhile, the left hemisphere is dominant, logical, analytical, and rational.

Personality is a key factor in understanding human behavior.

It reflects how an individual feels, thinks, and acts, influencing every activity they engage in. Personality is shaped by family, home, school or work, culture, climate, religion, friends, acquaintances, environment, language, beliefs, and so on. Genes also play a fundamental role in personality development, which researchers agree is...

- Temperament: The emotional nature of an individual, something you are born with.

- Character: Acquired affective-dynamic traits that are inherited.
- Attitudes: Persistent predispositions to respond to a situation.
- Constitution: External aspects, the origin of functional reactions.
- Aptitude: The ability to do something.
- Traits: Constant characteristics of behavior.

Aspects of Personality:

- Private self = Psychocorporal image.
- Social self = Influenced by others' opinions.
- Ideal self = What we wish to be.
- Real self = The true personality.

Personality in the face of loss can trigger psychological and psychosomatic trauma, which impacts emotions and sensations both in the short and long term, at physical, emotional, and psychological levels. Seeking physical well-being amidst emotional pain is a personal responsibility, encouraging individuals to relieve symptoms without prolonging survival, anxiety, agony, suffering, stress, or grief in the face of any loss.

The challenge is to improve life and commit to the great responsibility of ONESELF, in finding the satisfaction needed to live and die with dignity. This can only be achieved if resources are effectively channeled to confront life and all that comes with losses, right up until death, thus achieving emotional balance, and a state of harmony and mental peace.

Losses and grief confront us with inevitable suffering, which is often magnified into feelings of helplessness, abandonment, discouragement, and isolation. It's also evident that this can worsen physical pain, which is often a component of illness. It's important to note that talking about death requires reflection on the individual's personality and their needs. Letting go of attachment can be seen as resistance to change, which may manifest as anger, fear, resentment, frustration, vulnerability, sorrow, criticism, rejection, and guilt. These feelings together invite us to turn inward and confront the "ego".

Thus, the process of facing death and loss is deeply tied to emotions, frustrations, fantasies, mental representations, destructive thoughts, and behaviors linked to the loss of health, suffering, and pain. Human beings are bound to a series of phenomena, including psychological, psychosocial, and even economic factors, which are set in motion, culminating in death.

When one observes what has been lived and what has been lost, when "everything" is taken away, dreams, projects, the will to live, the breath of peace, tranquility, and well-being that comes from what has been achieved in life—parents, siblings, education, partners, children, hopes, work, enthusiasm, freedom, euphoria, love, faith, and dreams... and suddenly... A great silence. Because in feeling that vast emptiness, in experiencing the loss, comes the pain of the soul, the emotional pain, and the physical pain.

Since death is a cultural concept and its representations depend on a belief system, it is also true that it is what we avoid the most and are least willing to confront. Yet, it is the one thing we cannot escape, which is why it causes anxiety, fear, depression, anger, sadness, guilt, and rejection. The spiritual aspect plays a role in how we relate to a higher being, while the rational part understands that the person is no longer there. But the heart and the emotional part struggle to integrate this absence, which is why denial is so common in grief.

When asking the question, what would happen if I could know the date of my death? I am faced with the possibility of reconciling with life. I might travel, organize my unfinished business better, learn to do things differently, or would knowing when I will die really change the way I exist? Would it lead me to make peace with my choices, or create a sense of urgency to live more fully?

It's better to understand that death can be the greatest ally to the way we live, as if it were our best friend, encouraging us to reflect on our existence in this life.

Giving Meaning to Life in the Face of Losses

Focus on what you have, not on what is missing.

Chapter 2
Grief

Sigmund Freud was the first to develop a theory of grief, where he investigated that suffering is due to attachment.

The goal of grief is to detach feelings and attachments from the lost object. In this sense, grief or mourning is a normal process; however, when discussing melancholy, it refers to pathological grief.

For Thanatodynamics, which means: *Thánatos*, "Death, loss," and *Dynamis*, "the study of the laws and causes that govern movement," according to Fernando R. Gómez Urrea, grief never fully closes. Instead, it only transmutes its symbolic meanings, signifiers, abstractions, and implications.

Grief, in general, is an emotional and active process, not a state. It is a step toward adapting to losses: the death of a loved one, family members, friends, work, or material things, a significant object or event. This process involves physical, emotional, familial, behavioral, social, and spiritual reactions that every human being is exposed to.

For Thanatology, a human science whose meaning is: *Thánatos*, "study of death," and *Logos*, "treatise/study," it is ironically a part of life. After living, one always dies. Thanatology is defined as a science that helps with dying well, and I would also add, living well by giving meaning to life. From the point of view of Thanatology, the process of loss is understood in terms of time, suggesting a normal period for resolution and proposing various classifications.

Variants of Grief

Anticipatory Grief: This occurs when one anticipates the death of a loved one or even their own death, often after a terminal illness diagnosis, preparing for the farewell. There is an intense emotional burden. For example, when the sudden news comes that a loved one has been in an accident and is facing death. Simply living with a chronic-degenerative illness or an irreversible disability can alter life plans.

Grief in Professional Practice: This pertains to the attachments, expectations, and needs one seeks to fulfill. It becomes complicated to fill the void caused by the loss or what the lost object represents for the person.

Posthumous Normal Grief: This is conventional grief, where it is expected that the person will succumb to a chronic degenerative illness. For instance, someone diagnosed with dementia or Alzheimer's, or even the case of a child who won't develop according to their chronological age.

Delayed Grief: This occurs when, at the time of the loss, the need to be strong or feeling overwhelmed by everything happening in the moment prevents the person from grieving. An example would be dealing with the stressful situations following the death of a loved one who passed away far from their home country, requiring numerous legal procedures to have the body returned.

Chronic grief: when attachments are intensified in the face of loss, and denial remains for an indefinite period, causing individuals to continue behaving as if the person were still present, or significant dates constantly trigger pain again and again for months and years. Example: in cases of sudden death, guilt may arise for not having said or done something to prevent it, or in some cases, when unresolved conflicts or discomfort existed.

Perinatal and neonatal grief: the expectations of life-hope are affected, and guilt arises from the mother's fantasy, thinking that it was due to not eating well, sexual activity, movements that caused the death, or excessive work.

Grief due to abortion: feelings of failure may arise for not having taken care of oneself to prevent it, or for not having done the right thing to ensure the baby's birth.

Complicated grief: when adaptation after loss is inadequate, it interferes with personal, work, or school matters, relocation, moving to another country, friendships, school, and it can be associated with psychiatric problems in adulthood.

Absence grief: this can be related to a person, object, event, or situation, experienced by someone who has lost something to which they belonged, resulting in longing—the need to feel the warmth, the smell, the voice of a loved one, or the absence of physical contact. In other words, it is the absence of what the other person, situation, or thing represented in their life.

Special Types of Grief

Grief due to an unexpected death (sudden death or suicide): It requires more time for processing.

Grief caused by an accident: It is important to say goodbye to the deceased and view the body (this depends on the person).

Grief due to death by crime: An aggravating factor will be the impotent rage toward the murderer, the absence of justice, or anger against God for allowing this to happen.

Grief due to disaster: caused by natural events such as tsunamis, earthquakes, hurricanes, floods, fires, volcanic eruptions, extreme temperatures, among others. There is a clear awareness of the vulnerability of life, and it includes impact, shock, flashbacks, survivor's guilt, feelings of confusion, and emotional numbness. It causes greater anger and powerlessness when the catastrophe is man-made, leading to a loss of basic trust in the world.

Grief due to pandemics: those who experience it suffer a farewell without closure, ritual, or family.

Grief without a body: this happens when the body does not appear, and the search is declared over, as in cases of theft, kidnapping, airplane or maritime accidents, or natural disasters.

Grief due to suicide: if secrecy is chosen, the incongruence with reality will affect behavior and communication, and interpretations that trigger symptoms will arise.

Grief due to the death of a child: an illogical death, it likely encompasses the greatest pain due to what it symbolizes, as it is expected that, according to chronological order, parents would die first. It leaves a void, devastating depending on the nature of the death and expectations. *What do I do with my anger...? And toward God... What does it mean to lose a child? Why mine?*

The more we love, the more it hurts when they die (we distance ourselves from reality). It paralyzes the possibility of a future... The future of *my* child, through him, and with it, the expectations of life.

Children ask: *"What? Am I going to die?"* And what do we tell them?

Pathological Grief: It transforms into major depressive disorder or adjustment disorder. It is a long process, not linear, with relapses or setbacks. It is important to assess the person to understand what stage they are in and encourage them to focus on what they have rather than what they have lost. Additionally, the personal meaning of life and growth must be redefined. It involves denial and can trigger any mental illness, even leading to thoughts of not wanting to live.

Grief due to physical transcendence: It invites awareness of the fact that one is going to die, completely changing one's entire perspective on life. It is easier to think about the implications than to live them, and even more so to overcome them. The loss is felt when expectations of development are generated, which can be disrupted upon hearing the news of the decline in physical strength and functions, especially if it involves some form of bodily disarticulation.

The way one has lived in their body impacts how one can accept and regulate emotions. No one can drive a body except the one who lives in it.

Grief due to cultural belonging: Cultural grief generates several losses:

- Loss of traditions
- Loss of language
- Loss of education
- Loss of entertainment

In culture, there is an environment of isolation, the purest expression of unwanted loneliness, a kind of collective suicide, a social depression to which we are captive through culture, especially those who have changed their cultural environment by living in a new country or territorial entity.

It is not only the territory that is lost but also the language, the music, the act of singing those old songs, playing the games, and the customs and traditions of a people. It demoralizes the sense of home, trust, and freedom, trapping one in work. It becomes oppressive when remembering what has been lost.

Losing the habits of social interaction is losing the culture of belonging, and loneliness, as well as a lack of adaptation, emerges.

Stopping the cultivation of social life sooner or later forces one to become a foreigner in the place they inhabit.

There are those who, upon failing to integrate into that place, exert violence upon themselves through self-destructive habits and behaviors, which in the worst cases, lead to suicidal tendencies or even the act itself.

The human being is an open system in continuous flow, movement, and transformation. It is important that survivors have "memories" of moments lived with the deceased and family activities to give new meaning to the loss.

Communication with oneself is a formative path; it allows one to release destructive thoughts, stress, and tensions, increases strength, processes frustrations, feeds the intellect, nurtures reason, sparks motivational engines, exercises memory, or develops spirituality.

TRANSCENDENCE

What does the ego want to live?
What does the heart want to live?
What does the spirit want to live?

In communication, when one sits down and asks, *who wants to exist or rule my life?*, there are authors who mention that normal grief lasts from 6 months to a year, as the first year contains many significant dates that will bring the absence of the lost one to the surface, confronting social and emotional grief.

Stages of Grief

When discussing thanatology, we cannot overlook the stages of grief. Elisabeth Kübler-Ross states that the process of pain is always accompanied by a feeling of anger, and people often choose to suppress this feeling, with the predominant attitude toward death being one of rejection.

1. Denial and isolation: A defense mechanism that, after some time, is replaced by acceptance.

2. Anger: When the denial phase can no longer be maintained, it is replaced by feelings of anger towards oneself, God, and everything else.
3. Bargaining: An attempt to postpone the inevitable, creating a deadline, with feelings such as abandonment and loneliness.
4. Depression: When the terminally ill patient can no longer deny their insensitivity or stoicism, their anger and rage will soon be replaced by a great sense of loss.
5. Acceptance: Kübler-Ross says that there are patients who fight until the end; these patients may not be able to reach acceptance with peace and dignity.

Jorge Bucay, a physician and Gestalt psychotherapist, outlines seven stages in the grief process:

1. Disbelief: A moment of denial, where there is no pain, and the surprise leads to confusion. The more unexpected the death, the deeper the confusion and disbelief will be.
2. Regression: A painful explosion; emotions surface uncontrollably, preventing communication.
3. Anger: Directed at those considered responsible for the death—towards God, life, others, and even the deceased. It places us in reality and prepares the body for sadness.
4. Guilt: I direct resentment toward myself for not having prevented the death and blame myself for what I didn't do when I had the chance.
5. Desolation: Sadness, helplessness, the realization that there is nothing we can do. We experience loneliness, sadness that hurts physically, and may even have strange sensations and perceptions, such as pseudo-hallucinations.

Fertility: Transforming the energy tied to pain into action.

Acceptance: It involves separating, distinguishing oneself from the person who died. Acceptance means internalizing; I realize that what that person gave me can be transcended but not forgotten. In some cases, patients experience these stages alternately.

Denial and isolation

Anger
Bargaining } Closing circles
Depression
Acceptance

Intervention Process (Coping) for Grief and Loss

Grief and Loss Process

Grief is something that only the individual can do for themselves.

- Examine: Acknowledge the loss, admit the death, and understand that it is necessary to explore what one feels, and find the gain despite the loss in both thinking and feeling.
- Reorganize: Reorganize thoughts and feelings, express emotions, and give new meaning to what has been lost.
- Relive feelings: In a realistic way, to achieve a sense of balance regarding the loss, perhaps even commemorating the loss and what it represents.
- Modify values and priorities: Shift the values and priorities from the previous way of living.
- Adapt: Adapt to a new life by replacing the physical relationship with the nostalgia of memories.

Thanatology: Supports the journey to improve quality of life. For example, assisting a dying person and their family members, through the support of doctors and healthcare professionals, in facing grief over death. It begins with illnesses and moves through various processes.

A person structures their concept of death using tools, defense mechanisms, reactions, adaptive tactics, and resolution strategies for grief and other types of loss, which result in human behavior responses from their development.

Culturally, the news of death comes to us as something negative, as a new dimension of life, producing uncertainty and fear.

Giving Meaning to Life in the Face of Losses

We suffer because of what we love, and love is constructive by nature. The way to prevent that suffering from damaging our physical and spiritual life is to return to its roots, transforming it into constructive energy.

Rebuilding oneself would be the first task, and, out of love, finding a way to give meaning to that pain.

It is important to consider that during the grieving process, after caring for someone with an illness or enduring days of anguish, many debts are left with the body: sleepless days and nights, anxiety, extreme nervous tension, poor alignment, and mental exhaustion from seeking answers and solutions. This affects health, exposing individuals to all kinds of psychosomatic illnesses that could become chronic, such as gastritis, colitis, or anxiety.

In cases of unexpected deaths, the mental and emotional aggression received can be compared to an explosion inside the body. Uncontrollable hormone surges circulate through the bloodstream, and conflicting and confusing thoughts tear at the mind, leading to extreme physical and psychological exhaustion.

Talking about the loss means feeling the absence of the interaction, relationship, or connection with what has been lost.

If I lose a loved one, I cry (as one of many reactions).

I cry for the absence and the emptiness felt from no longer having that relationship. One also cries for the absence of that connection.

There is also the painful sensation of no longer being the person you once were, stemming from the loss. For example, does a mother cease to be a mother when she loses her child?

Therefore, what is mourned and what is lost needs to be redefined in an open system of continuous transformation and movement that life offers.

When should I seek help?

It is important to consult a medical professional, spiritual guide, support group leader, or mental health professional when symptoms such as the following appear:

- Anxiety, insomnia
- Recurrent thoughts of guilt
- Suicidal thoughts
- Pessimistic outlook on the future
- Destructive thoughts
- Restlessness or prolonged depression
- Feeling of chest tightness
- Repressed or uncontrollable anger
- Lack of concentration, becoming non-functional

Accompaniment

Accompaniment shows us the adaptation that, sooner or later, leads us to relinquish the prolonged suffering caused by the absence.

Additionally, it has the capacity to harmonize the individual with their surroundings and establish levels of functionality and dysfunctionality through therapeutic actions. It addresses the origin, belonging, and transcendence of their process, according to Fernando Gómez, who explains it in his postulates:

"Re" (to return to: remember, recognize, and rebuild).

When one wins oneself over, they can no longer carry the loss of the other, because there is no other. For example, when experiencing loneliness—understood as the lack of company—one stops feeling alone without being alone.

One does not experience loneliness in what is gained; loneliness is only felt in what is lost.

When one clings to not being abandoned, they abandon themselves even more.

When one clings to not experiencing loneliness, they feel more alone. When one clings to freedom, they are less free.

When one accepts abandonment, loneliness, and freedom, they win themselves over.

It aids in adaptation and the discovery of paths for development. Therefore, Thanatology cannot die, it only transforms, and now finds in Thanatodynamics another way to process death; it is the counterpart, the polarity, and the complement of Thanatology in order to process losses.

There can be no joy in reunion without suffering the pain of farewell!

Thanatodynamics helps in the development of a person's life in the face of losses. Its function is to establish a strategic path for adaptation, offering an option for intervention. It formally explores the history and implications that shaped how someone reacts to losses, as well as examines the relationship a human being has with their environment and how the latter influences their development when faced with losses, including death.

Transforming Pain
Thanatologist-Patient Relationship

The benefit of Thanatology is to soothe, calm, and alleviate the pain caused by death, loss, illness, and despair, improving the quality of life for the patient, their family, and the medical staff. It develops three key areas: clinical care, education and training of professionals, and research.

The thanatologist has several places where they can carry out their work: the hospital, the patient's home, or their office. It is important to emphasize that the best place for caring for a chronic or terminally ill patient is their home.

The actions a thanatologist can take include: establishing empathy, being sensitive and humane, recognizing the patient's needs, and, if the patient is in their final moments, recognizing the needs of the family as well. The strategy might involve relaxation, hypnosis, addressing unresolved matters, discussing the patient's needs and beliefs, mediating between the patient and family, managing and expressing fears, and helping them find the meaning of life.

On the other hand, the characteristics of the thanatologist include having a loving attitude, offering accompaniment without overstepping boundaries. The best place to take a dying person is their home, reducing emergency hospitalizations, ensuring the patient receives basic needs, helping with family cooperation, maintaining the patient's cleanliness and hygiene, and ensuring mobilization to prevent bedsores and pulmonary complications.

Finally, the goal of Thanatology is to improve quality of life, referring to the level of satisfaction and functioning. The value placed on what is considered quality of life depends on each individual.

According to the World Health Organization, every person has the right to live to their fullest physical, emotional, psychological, spiritual, social, and occupational potential; to be treated as an independent, alert human being; to express emotions and feelings; to have relief from suffering; to be cared for by sensitive professionals; to not have their suffering prolonged; to not die alone; to die without pain and with dignity.

The memory of love prevails in the heart.

Chapter 3
The Enigma of Death

Death is the mystery of life, the only certainty that human beings possess. Therefore, it is likely the greatest pain one can experience in the face of losing a loved one. It brings about the separation of body and soul after a deep slumber. It is nothing more than a temporary step. In this sense, death is, in reality, the day of birth. Death marks the boundary; it puts an end to the drive to dominate life, regardless of age, religion, social status, or place. Each person has their moment of life and death.

It generates incomprehension, fear, anguish, bitterness, insecurity, helplessness, perplexity, rejection, grief, desolation, dismay, despair, and countless other afflictions.

Human fragility is right there before us: the issue of time, illness, natural disasters, war, and the unexpected. Families struggle between… hiding the truth or letting the sick person find out.

It is important to note that there are different types of death:

- **Death of an embryo or fetus:** The child conceived in the mind but never materialized; singleness, celibacy, sexual preference, or infertility.
- **Anticipated death:** Resulting from a terminal illness, the pain is the same, but perhaps the preparation for the illness process helps. It may involve anticipatory grief, but there is always the hope for a miracle, the sign of life that returns hope—like when the body seems to recover, only to gather strength before finally dying. Imagining with terror how the end will be. Memories flood in, and emotions mix between pain, hope, triumph, relapses, and the option to remember "they were brave in their illness."
- **Abruptly death:** Without any prior symptoms, as in the case of a heart attack, stroke, or aneurysm. There are also accidental deaths, heart attacks, homicides, natural disasters, and fatal accidents.
- **Sudden death:** One day they were talking, eating with you, and suddenly, silence came. Perhaps you're trapped in anger, asking, *Why them?* Other times, there is guilt for all the things left unsaid or undone. And the most difficult question: *Where did I go wrong?*
- **Unexpected death:** The mental and emotional assault received is comparable to an explosion inside our bodies, with uncontrollable hormone surges coursing through our bloodstream, and conflicting, confusing thoughts tearing at our minds, leading to extreme physical and psychological exhaustion.
- **Death by suicide**: Possibly one of the clearest expressions of human suffering, despair, and helplessness. "Suicide" and "suicidal" refer to a voluntary behavior. As a goal, it seeks to cause one's own death or is a way of expressing or communicating feelings of despair, helplessness, or frustration.

The death of many dreams, illusions, and expectations often does not receive adequate grief work.

Culturally, we are taught about death: *We must fear and respect it. We should not speak about it. It can be a reward or a punishment. It's better not to invoke it.*

Love is as strong as death. Specialists have defined grief as the normal process that follows the loss of a loved one. During grief, love continues, and it is possible to remain connected with the loved one during and even after grieving.

- We mourn the absence, the death of the other.
- When a spouse dies, one becomes a widow or widower.
- When parents die, one becomes an orphan.
- But when a child dies… there is no name for that.

We cannot ignore the importance of religion in recognizing how it influences behavior.

Regarding the legal framework, it is important to know that there are normative frameworks where we will find rights and obligations.

The Child in the Face of Death

A child will react according to what is presented in their environment. If the death was sudden, violent, or slow, it is important how the news is handled in an effort to protect the child from suffering. Efforts might be made to prevent the child from seeing the pain and to avoid causing distress, even to the point of isolating them from the situation or offering a substitute to distract them from reality. Sometimes, the explanation of a loved one's death can confuse the child. For example: *"Grandpa was very tired and died"* or *"Grandma just fell asleep."*

The reaction will depend on the child's age and degree of attachment, whether to a parent, sibling, toy, pet, blanket, pillow, etc. Their education, cultural and religious teachings also play a role. For instance: *"Grandpa went to be with God,"* or the attitudes they have learned and observed, such as feelings of sadness or guilt for getting sick, often framed by expressions like: *"It's cold, cover up, if you get sick, it's your fault."*

But what happens when an adult has to struggle with their own beliefs about the terrible nature of the death of a child or son/daughter? The child senses what is happening to the body, though they may not understand the meaning, they can feel it.

It is wrong to teach a child that if they behave well, they will go to heaven, but if not, to hell.

In the child's experience, religious belief can offer comfort with the notion of a *"kind God welcoming you with open arms."*

However, if God is not part of the belief system, the child should not feel abandoned either.

The way the news is delivered to the child, or how they perceive it, can lead to confusion with questions like: If Mom or Dad dies, who will take care of me?" or "Did I make them angry and they died?" or "If I die, will I go to be with Grandpa?" "Depending on how these questions are handled, the consequences may include depression, anxiety, hyperactivity, anger, guilt, a sense of vulnerability and personal insecurity, behavioral problems, and sleep or attention and concentration disorders.

The child's age is crucial when facing loss and grief. In terms of their understanding, the variations are as follows:

In their first year, they explore their surroundings and objects that are not in sight. These are not in their mind yet, but they can distinguish between their mother and other people.

At 2 years old, they begin the process of separation and individuation.

Children have magical and fantasy thinking, which they cannot distinguish from reality, perceiving death as a *"separation"* from their loved ones or the objects they are attached to. The pain is not prolonged but can be intense and temporary at the same time.

Starting at the age of 6, children may perceive death as a punishment for bad behavior, with religious, cultural, and familial consequences becoming evident. This is the stage where they start questioning what might happen after death. It is common to see feelings of guilt arise during grief. They confuse fantasy with reality.

From 6 to 12 years old, they have a greater ability to perceive reality; however, they assess guilt based on the severity of the harm caused. They view death more in terms of causes and are often curious about what happens after death. Feelings of guilt, repressed anger, hatred, anxiety, disorganized behavior, sleep disorders, lack of concentration, tension, vulnerability, isolation, insecurity, behavioral problems, and disciplinary issues may emerge, especially if they feel they had something to do with the death. For example, if their parents argue about their schooling, and one of them falls ill and dies.

If a child becomes stuck in the loss, there is a risk that they may stop developing psychologically and behave like a younger child.

The reaction to the death of a sibling can range from no response at all to the presence of nightmares, aggression, and somatic problems. There may be a decline in school performance, anxiety, depression, worry about responsibility, feelings of guilt, resentment toward parents for spending too much time with the sibling, fear that their parents or they themselves might die, and recurring fantasies about death.

The Adolescent in the Face of Death

Adolescents may be able to better cope with the consequences of death, depending on their emotional development, age, the quality of their personal relationships, and their level of maturity. Feeling isolated, they may confront and reject the values of their family group violently in an effort to feel free.

Symptoms to watch for in an adolescent: depression, sleep disturbances, eating disorders, impatience, low self-esteem, sudden changes in school performance, and deterioration in family or friend relationships. Destructive behaviors may include alcohol and drug abuse, fighting, engaging in unprotected sexual activity, denial of pain, and displays of strength and maturity. They often idealize the deceased loved one and may seek reassurance from doctors about their own health, possibly even attempting to replace the lost loved one. This can even trigger a complicated personality in adulthood. However, when faced with their own death, they still hold onto hope for recovery.

With the adolescent, it is necessary to work on the disruption of their personal life, sexuality, life plans, and their feelings of despair and anger in the face of this reality.

The Adult in the Face of Death

Their thoughts are more influenced by personal, social, and cultural factors. For example: losing a job, the sudden death of a spouse, or contracting a serious illness. These events produce significant stress and require a reorganization of the individual's personal and social life. Adulthood can be divided into three stages:

- Young adult: 21 to 35 years old.
- Middle adult: 36 to 45 years old.
- Mature adult: 46 to 60 years old.

As an adult, it is important to become aware of what it means to die:

- Illogical moment: It comes when it is least wanted.
- Moment of transcendence: It gives meaning to life (a transition from one state to another).
- Process that begins at birth: From the umbilical cord, when we are born we breathe, and when we die, we stop breathing.
- Period of separation of body and mind.
- A time marked by the absence of vital signs.
- End of life.

The most frequent symptoms in adults include: mood changes, alterations in eating and sleeping habits, compulsive use of addictive substances, social isolation, negative thoughts and recurrent ideas of death, and behaviors that put their lives at risk, among others.

Old Age in the Face of Death

In old age, one needs a deeper connection with spirituality and a clearer definition of their beliefs. The elderly face the following crises: aging, fatigue, and exhaustion. Significant people in their lives begin to pass away, and there is a decline in physical and mental faculties, considering all the morphological, physiological, biochemical, and psychological changes. They may feel alone or desolate, endure suffering, and face the proximity of death. If the transition into old age is harmonious, we will find an elderly person filled with wisdom, calm, serene, and with a sense of existential purpose.

COMMON FEARS:

- Losing a loved one
- Seeing them suffer (they are sedated, but you are not)
- Feeling fear and uncertainty
- Being unable to help them
- Being unable to be near them
- Not acting correctly
- Being unable to tell the truth
- Insufficient finances to pay
- An unpredictable future
- Loneliness
- Helplessness
- Inadequate treatment
- Showing their fears
- Not being strong enough
- Not being able to participate in the care of their sick loved one

The fears of adults are often passed on to their children.

In the mystery of life and death, there is fear of dying. Therefore, the invitation is to think more about living. Just as waking is the end of sleeping, death is not the issue—it is the fear of death. "Learning not to fear one's own fear."

A light amid the darkness of pain is often found in God. However, we still seek an explanation for pain. Despite everything, suffering opens the door to hope, with its foundation rooted in faith.

Emotional Manifestations

- Difficulty understanding
- Anxiety: Insecurity leading up to a panic attack
- Repressed anger: A natural effect of any absence
- Denial: Attempts to persist in the relationship; it is normal to fantasize about "attachment objects"
- Self-reproach: Insignificant acts as a form of self-punishment
- Guilt: Comfort found in the idea that someone else's death occurred instead of one's own, even to the extent of feeling that they should have died instead of the loved one
- Personalization phenomena: Adopting traits, qualities, gestures, characteristics, or peculiarities of the loved one
- Sensation of the deceased's presence: Causes illusions or hallucinations, hearing the loved one's voice or even feeling their presence

It is important to develop strategies to help an individual cope with loss.

According to Worden, first, the reality of the loss must be accepted, followed by working through the emotions and pain associated with it. Then, the person must adapt to an environment where the deceased is absent (around three months later). Finally, the individual must emotionally relocate the deceased and continue living.

Pain, even without words, wounds both emotionally
and physically in the face of loss.

Chapter 4
Pain

The International Association for the Study of Pain defines pain as *"an unpleasant sensory and emotional experience associated with actual or potential tissue damage."* The perception of pain involves a sensory neuronal system (nociceptors) and afferent nerve pathways that respond to nociceptive tissue stimuli. Nociception can be influenced by other factors, such as physical symptoms, psychological problems, social and cultural factors, and spiritual conflicts.

It is important to know and be aware that the pain of life can be very similar to the pain of death, but that pain can be short-lived if we reframe it or manage to replace it with another feeling. The comfort or faith in being better in another realm with a divine being, a creator who will take away that pain.

For a proper assessment of pain, it is advisable to understand several aspects, such as its temporal variation (acute, chronic), pathogenesis, and intensity.

Pain Variants

Pain is classified into different types, and this can be done based on its duration, pathogenesis, location, course, intensity, factors, and prognosis for pain control.

Based on duration, it can be acute or chronic.

Acute: Generally, acute pain starts suddenly and is of short duration. Intense pain can cause tachycardia, increased respiratory rate and blood pressure, sweating, and pupil dilation, with minimal psychological component. Examples include hollow organ perforation, neuropathic pain, and musculoskeletal pain related to pathological fractures.

Chronic: Unlimited in duration, it is defined as persistent pain lasting several days, weeks, or more. It is accompanied by a psychological component and is the typical pain in cancer patients.

Based on pathogenesis (i.e., causes, processes, and disease development):

Neuropathic pain: Caused by direct stimulation of the central nervous system or by injury to peripheral nerve pathways. It is described as stabbing or burning pain, accompanied by paresthesias, dysesthesias, hyperalgesia, hyperesthesia, and allodynia. Examples of neuropathic pain include brachial or lumbosacral plexopathy post-irradiation, peripheral neuropathy post-chemotherapy and/or post-radiotherapy, and spinal cord compression.

Nociceptive pain: The most common type, divided into somatic and visceral pain.

Psychogenic pain: The psycho-social environment surrounding the individual plays a role. This type typically involves a constant need for increasing doses of analgesics with little efficacy.

Somatic pain: Produced by abnormal excitation of superficial or deep somatic nociceptors, causing aching or gnawing pain, as seen in bone metastases, post-surgical incision pain, and musculoskeletal pain.

Localized pain, sharp and radiating along nerve pathways. The most common is bone pain caused by bone metastases. Treatment should include a nonsteroidal anti-inflammatory drug (NSAID).

Deafferentation pain: Depends on peripheral nervous system injuries, resulting from compression or inflammation of peripheral nerves or the spinal cord, or from trauma or chemical injuries to peripheral nerves caused by surgery, radiation, or chemotherapy for cancer.

Visceral pain: Caused by abnormal excitation of visceral nociceptors. This pain is continuous and deep, described as "squeezing" or "pressure" pain, caused by infiltration, compression, distension, or stretching of the viscera. It may be accompanied by nausea and vomiting and can radiate to areas distant from its origin. Frequently, it is associated with neurovegetative symptoms. Examples include colicky pain, liver metastases, and pancreatic cancer. This pain responds well to opioid treatment.

Continuous pain: Persistent throughout the day and does not go away.

Breakthrough pain: A transient exacerbation of pain in patients who otherwise have well-controlled, stable background pain. Incidental pain is a subtype of breakthrough pain induced by movement or vol**untary action by the patient.**

Iatrogenic pain due to radiation: A multifactorial pain that requires appropriate treatment to minimize disruptions in proposed therapeutic regimens. Medications that reduce the toxicity of treatment regimens involving irradiation are necessary.

Based on intensity or course, pain can be categorized as:

Mild: Allows for regular activities.

Moderate: Interferes with normal activities and requires treatment with minor opioids.

Severe: Interferes with rest and requires major opioids.

Pain can be superficial, sharp, burning, deep, or oppressive.

The biological pain variables mentioned above are important to monitor, in order to prevent worsening symptoms.

Family pain: Due to the sense of belonging—*"my"* child, parents, siblings, etc.—the pain is magnified. In such cases, assertive communication, where thoughts, feelings, and actions align, can help, including active listening to foster empathy without judgment. By speaking about it, healing begins.

Social pain: Due to one's way of being or belonging, it is necessary to transform these feelings—such as hatred, apathy, or fear—into something beneficial.

Psychological pain: Emotions play a very important role, as they relate to expectations, hopes, or emotional dependencies. Confronting them helps separate fear, anger, and sadness, allowing for boundaries to be set and enabling a person to be functional again, regaining identity, confidence, love, and self-assurance.

Spiritual pain: Faith, trust, and spiritual support help alleviate the pain of the soul.

The pain of time: Often, we find ourselves stuck in the past, which causes pain, and overcoming it is difficult because it is based on memories that sustain the need not to feel the absence or the loss. Paradoxically, talking about the future can also cause pain, rooted in uncertainty, because there is no certainty about what will happen.

However, when talking about emotional pain, it is crucial to identify the emotional state in order to investigate how to control the pain and avoid possible somatization.

In this way, pain is a sensation that affects our body in a localized and defined manner. It is a localized physical discomfort that results in an unpleasant sensory and emotional experience, associated with actual or potential physical harm, which tends to subside with chemical or emotional relief... *when you acknowledge the pain of your soul.*

And your silent pains? How do they speak through your body? Illness is not bad; it warns . you that... you are on the wrong path!

Nelson Torres, Doctor of Psychiatry (UCV) and expert in Psychoneuroimmunolinguistics, says: *"The body screams what the mouth keeps silent."*

"Illness is a conflict between the personality and the soul," — Bach.

Pain is addiction — Suffering is psychological and spiritual (cultural).

In every loss, there is a gain, and finding that gain through pain brings us into contact with the feelings and the emptiness left by what is no longer there.

(Perhaps my value) daughter-orphan.

Pain is silent and solitary (guilt).

Through pain, death is accepted, and one transcends.

Our body and soul hurt because the human being is one, and the pain that surfaces with loss and death shakes the human being in their entirety.

There is great pain generated by the anguish of not finding something valuable.

he shock produced by bad news, where the first thing lost is peace, presses on the chest; it causes severe headaches, emptiness in the stomach, tightness in the throat, dry mouth, sleep disturbances, and appetite changes.

Classification of pain

- Physical (body)
- Nociceptive somatic visceral (chemical, physical, biological)

- Central or peripheral neuropathic pain
- Emotional pain: Occurs when the value system (of the soul) is broken, including religious, aesthetic, moral or ethical, and economic values.

Different types of pain:

- Psychological: The personality hurts.
- Biological/physical: The body hurts.
- Spiritual: What one desires, thinks, and overthinks hurts.
- Social: How one is seen hurts (criticism, rejection, guilt).
- Emotional: The soul hurts.

How to deal with pain?

Physical pain of the body: Address the cause, improve with exercise, proper nutrition, and rest through good sleep. It invites reflection on what *my* body is telling me (e.g., cold, colitis, gastritis, pneumonia, etc.).

Emotional pain of the soul: Hope and living day by day bring joy in the present (this helps); pain is not evil in itself, it is a signal inviting reflection on what I am thinking, which will affect my emotions. For example: thinking negatively about the future leads to feelings of anger, and it's likely that the symptom generated will be anxiety.

When there is inner pain due to memories, it manifests outwardly through a symptom. For example: headaches, muscle pain, etc.; the attitude that follows is likely irritability or a sense of anxiety.

Suffering produces deep, existential questions. The emotional remedy is an analgesic that can be created through family unity and communication as a foundation to foster trust, stability, and love, providing self-assurance.

Is there pain in natural death?

When we understand that pain is a warning mechanism in which the brain signals the individual about the possibility of imminent or existing harm, or malfunction in the body, it is designed for the individual to take this into account and seek help.

"Natural" death occurs when the person passes away, and their heart and lungs simply stop functioning, causing a cardiorespiratory arrest. When the heart stops pumping blood, oxygen stops flowing to the lungs, and thus breathing ceases, these are the mechanisms that keep us alive, and then all other systems shut down. If all systems shut down, there can be no sensations of any kind because the centers in the brain that inform the body of pain also stop functioning. If there is no illness causing pain, there -theoretically- should be no pain in those final moments of death; it is more like a sensation of deep sleep and a descent into a spiral of light.

Pain in the case of illness occurs before death, but not at the moment of death. Accurate studies indicate that the brain is programmed to block severe pain (such as from suffocation or burns), and after approximately 30 seconds, it is blocked, and nothing is felt anymore.

The gain from pain is being in touch with the feelings and the emptiness left by what is no longer there (perhaps my value) after the loss of parents and feeling like an orphaned daughter.

Pain is silent and solitary, and it can generate guilt. Through pain, death is accepted, and one transcends.

Factors that cause pain

In grief, the pain is TOTAL (your entire life hurts), it is genuine, real, and intense, and there is no pill that can soothe it—only a sedative that helps you sleep, to avoid feeling or thinking. But upon waking, it's still there, reminding you of what is no longer yours, what you have lost. It is essential to understand that grief is a process, not a condition that a doctor can fix, and it is incomparable to other severe pains like headaches, fractures, intestinal pain, burns, or post-operative pain.

In the face of grief and illness, the loss of a loved one produces excessive stress, intense physical and emotional exhaustion, with organic and psychological ramifications (in the body and mind) that have been the subject of numerous studies. It has been proven that stress causes changes in blood pressure and heart rate, as well as infectious, inflammatory, and autoimmune diseases. Likewise, it is known that grief predisposes individuals to exacerbations of pre-existing illnesses and puts family members at greater risk for complications of previous illnesses or the onset of new ones.

Physiological Factors

These factors contribute to a higher risk of illness as a result of loss:

Ignoring the changes and symptoms that arise, such as being unable to sleep, experiencing distressing thoughts, or painful sensations like disbelief, restlessness, and recurrent thoughts that lead to guilt/punishment.

Changes in health routines (abandoning previous habits and gradually neglecting oneself).

Indifference to early signs of illness (the person may not pay attention to them, or in their belief system, they think it's just part of what they are going through).

Improper management or neglect of pre-existing illnesses such as diabetes (high blood sugar), hypertension (high blood pressure), etc.

Lack of the usual care they once had.

Emotional Factors

In terms of psychological pain, it helps to remember the life shared with the lost loved one as vividly as possible. There's a need to face the dynamic of questions such as what to do with their belongings, photos, or visiting places once shared with the loved one. The purpose is to help move forward, to separate and set the appropriate boundaries that distinguish the individual from the lost loved one, reaffirming personal identity and regaining self-confidence. This way, they avoid losing themselves with the death of their loved one.

As feelings arise, prolonged stress, guilt, repressed anger, fears, feelings of rejection, irritability, loneliness, despair, anxiety, distress, hatred, relief over the end of a complicated relationship, searching for the person in familiar places, sensing their presence, dreaming about them, disbelief and denial, frustration, sleep disturbances, fear of death, the desire for solitude, impatience, the urge for everything to end, fatigue, the continuous replay of events, helplessness, and powerlessness—these are all normal feelings during grief. Recognizing and expressing these feelings with loved ones reduces the pain and helplessness caused by the loss.

Suffering amplifies pain; suffering makes pain chronic, and the question, *"Why me?"* is linked to psychological pain, arising in the mind and not in reality, it is a fantasy. Several negative thoughts affect behavior, emotions, and concentration.

Suffering has a physical link through symptoms like thirst or even loss of consciousness, either conscious or unconscious.

It manifests as physical and emotional exhaustion, unhappiness, and existential emptiness, leading to questions, destructive thoughts, fears, anger, sorrow, frustration, anxiety, spiritual pain, and the sensation that God has abandoned the desires and hopes of each individual. As a defense mechanism, people try to avoid suffering, but it is inevitable because it is inherent to life.

Causal Factors of Suffering:

- The loss of a loved one
- A lost or unrequited love—trigger… *"Suicide"*
- Jealousy and envy
- Frustrations, disappointments, and injustices
- Mistakes made, feelings of guilt
- Somatic and mental illnesses
- Existential emptiness, etc.

How suffering is translated:

- Anguish: Threatens integrity
- Sadness

- Melancholy
- Loneliness
- Existential boredom – apathy towards life
- Sorrow
- Fear
- Depression
- Desperation (hopelessness)

Symptoms

The human body is a biological machine composed of more than 10 trillion cells with biochemical, genetic, physiological, and psychological complexity. Through its organs and tissues, it processes and stores physical and emotional experiences, beliefs, dreams, and fantasies, which in turn generate behaviors and transmit thoughts to others, mostly non-verbal, reflecting personality. Seeing, touching, hearing, and smelling are feelings and emotions—they are human bodily experiences with different levels of consciousness.

It is important to consider that during the grieving process, after being the primary caregiver during an illness, along with days of anguish or simply hearing the news of the loss, many conflicts arise within the body: sleepless days and nights, anxiety, nervous tension, maximum levels of stress, poor nutrition, and mental exhaustion from seeking answers, all of which affect health.

Symptoms in the face of loss, to name a few: disbelief, confusion, restlessness, waves of acute anxiety, repetitive thoughts that are difficult to shake, dry mouth, muscle weakness, crying, trembling, sleep problems, loss of appetite, cold and sweaty hands, nausea, diarrhea, yawning, palpitations, or dizziness.

It is necessary to recognize, express, and discuss these symptoms with family, friends, or specialists. Addressing the pain will help carry out the necessary actions to alleviate it.

Due to false belief systems, guilt, and cultural factors, attention to the body's condition is often ignored or underestimated. This is justified by the need to focus on work and care for others—everyone but oneself. Attention is given to what is happening outside the body, while impulses, feelings, and emotions are neglected, leading to the accumulation of stress, tension, and emotional discomforts, eventually resulting in psychosomatic illnesses. For example:

An organic dysfunction may arise due to excessive nervous tension, typical of someone who assumes significant responsibility.

Some people present themselves to others as strong, mature, and responsible, claiming to have overcome emotions such as fear, anger, or anxiety. They embed this in their self-concept, while those emotions they cannot consciously accept are expressed through illnesses; this becomes a habit not accepted in their conscious mind.

Psychosomatic illnesses can become chronic, such as gastritis, colitis, or anxiety. Common remedies for ulcers or headaches are merely palliative and may bring side effects.

Somatic problems do not come alone—they invite psychological disturbances caused by physical ailments: stomach issues reflect an inability to digest ideas, fear of the new.

Somatic issues may affect the skin, scalp, or cause facial paralysis.

They stem from resentment, envy, feelings of inferiority, and self-assertive attitudes, leading to psychological disturbances, interpersonal relationship issues, and social maladaptation.

When presenting with severe somatic conditions, the clinical traits that Bellak presents schematically describe five types of responses to illness or disability:

A "normal" reaction to anxiety or depression, which, however, soon diminishes and becomes a concern approximately proportional to the actual degree of the illness or disability.

An evasive reaction, expressed through a denial of the illness; an attitude of imperturbability that is often accompanied by excessive activity and false cheerfulness. This attitude frequently turns into depression with anxiety and manifests in disobedience to follow the doctor's instructions.

A reactive depression that may be prolonged and involves hypochondria.

A funneling of all existing anxieties into the new focus of concern. Sometimes, these patients, who are generally disturbed individuals, abandon their previous, more diffuse manifestations of disturbance, and therefore seem more docile.

Psychological disability: For example, when a patient who is physically capable of functioning socially and occupationally develops fears, symptoms, or attitudes that incapacitate them.

Such manifestations can be observed in some patients who have only suffered minor illnesses; however, they appear in their fullest expression in those who have experienced serious organic illnesses or severe disabilities, such as cancer, heart disease, tuberculosis, or amputations.

Definitive Separation from a Loved One or
A Different Way of Being Together

Chapter 5
Loss

Starting from What is Lost

What is Loss?

Bowly (1980) mentions that "Loss is one of the most painful experiences a human being can suffer."

Loss refers to any emotional bond, the experience of having had "something" that is no longer there, be it a child, partner, pet, friend, family member, job, health, etc. These are the manifestations of pain or resistance that appear in various ways. If the loss is physical, it refers to a threatening physical deterioration, whether from an illness that leads to disability, a chronic or degenerative illness without the possibility of rehabilitation, or a real threat to physical integrity. Likewise, it can refer to any absence, damage, or deprivation that affects personal, material, or symbolic resources.

The reaction to loss will depend on how it was caused. For example: death due to illness, homicide, suicide, loss of a limb, disability, destruction of home, property, or professional career, natural disasters like hurricanes, earthquakes, tsunamis, as well as losses caused by the dissolution of marriages, friendships, and other intimate relationships such as infidelity, divorce, or rape. These may be worsened by apathy, indifference, misunderstanding, or feelings of guilt, making the burden of anguish even heavier.

In many ways, one can become stuck in the grief cycle; these negative outcomes are common in cases of traumatic loss (for example, those involving harm to the body, such as physical assaults or rapes, including deaths caused by the effects of alcohol).

In the case of the death of a child, the parents and siblings are not only deprived of the child's presence but also of the future they had expected, which makes adaptation more difficult.

What Do I Lose When I Lose?

Losing what has been acquired brings feelings of abandonment or helplessness, which manifest as a natural and necessary process. It triggers an instinctive, involuntary, and unconscious adaptation. Feeling indifference, dispossession, and neglect causes the process to ignite the desire and will to explore the surroundings to satisfy development and achieve adaptation—this means gaining control over life. For example, the mother is an inherited loss, and the father is an acquired loss.

What is lost when the umbilical cord is cut? Security is lost, along with the need to feel accompanied in a comfortable zone, while leaving the womb and cutting the umbilical cord represents an adaptive physiological challenge to learn how to take in and transform life from the environment.

We must remember that the absence of a loved one creates a double grief: first, the physical absence of the other, and second, the symbolic absence of the self in the other. For example, my father represented *"my security and support"*, and thus, the loss brings about a "before, during, and after" of what I lose.

Loss in adolescents is experienced through intense feelings of anger, guilt, or betrayal in their emotional breakups, sometimes leading to significant depression.

This process of "detachment" tends to be gradual and often manifests more at the behavioral level.

The loss of a spouse when the relationship is fractured requires finding peaceful and cooperative ways of communicating, avoiding sabotage out of resentment or engaging in an *"ego war."* When one spouse decides to leave, it may be helpful to keep significant objects rather than get rid of them. Ultimately, both parties must process their grief. The one initiating the breakup often experiences guilt, while the other feels anger, betrayal, or displacement.

The loss of a professional role involves a series of stress factors. These losses often arise spontaneously (and unexpectedly) due to work accidents, layoffs, or early retirement, leaving people feeling betrayed and diminished by a loss that is not compensated for in any way. Job losses can trigger familiar patterns of grief. *"Layoffs"* are often accompanied by anger and defiance, with the sense that the decision was unfair. If not processed constructively, these feelings can escalate into financial stress and self-sabotage. A critical life cycle transition can leave one feeling inadequate, affecting security and self-esteem, which is reflected in levels of anger, depression, anxiety, and the risk of interpersonal violence. The situation may feel increasingly desperate, and unemployed individuals may come to think that others would be "better off without them."

Loss of the housewife role: This can be devastating. The grief over the loss of her role as a wife, in her domestic tasks, as the family budget administrator, and as a social organizer, which had been fundamental not only to her identity but also to her self-esteem, leads to emotional instability as a consequence.

Financial loss: Typically, no clear solution is in sight, and the fears and feelings of worthlessness bring about anger and anxiety.

Loss due to theft: Experiencing the dispossession of possessions brings frustration and a sense of defenselessness that emotionally affects the individual. It can also deepen beliefs and assumptions that, until that moment, had been sources of security.

Loss of a pet: This causes sadness, guilt, and confusion. Many adults try to minimize the impact of the loss without managing to alleviate the pain.

Loss of a home: Attachments to spaces like bedrooms, friends, and neighbors who are seen as family, or even businesses where friendships were formed and memories made, can have a short, medium, and long-term impact if one cannot negotiate well-being in the new home.

School losses: Due to changing school cycles or moving homes, these can generate uncertainty and lower self-esteem. However, to a certain extent, such losses are often compensated by the new possibilities of learning and forming new friendships.

Present-absent or absent-present loss: When a loved one is physically present but psychologically absent due to illness or addiction. Or when a loved one is absent but still present, as in cases of kidnapping or disappearance. Hope remains for a change or reappearance, but anger, guilt, or the feeling of abandoning them also arise. Not only is the loved one lost, but they are also lost as a member of the family system.

But when one loses security, peace of mind, well-being, self-esteem, dreams, ideals, and I would add fantasies, the feeling becomes destructive in the face of victimization and involuntary survival. Apathy, negativity, and pessimism take hold, and illnesses, tragedies, and misfortunes arise as a result of not having matured through the process of loss and deciding how to deal with what has been lost.

Giving Meaning to Life in the Face of Losses

Variants of Loss

Self-esteem
- Respect
- Self confidence
- Value
- Trust
- Faith

Safety
- Peace of Mind
- Estability
- Health

Material
- House
- Valuable objects
- Car
- Phone

Love
- Sibling
- Parent
- Family
- Pet
- Godparent

Social
- Friend
- Godparent
- Coworker
- School

External
- Robbery
- Accident
- Kidnaping
- Jail

Physical
- Health
- Eyesight
- Pregnancy
- Limb
- Burntmes

Expressing Emotions and Feelings

If we consider what Freud said, there exists a state of painful mood, a loss of interest in the external world, and a loss of the capacity to love (emotional impoverishment). Melancholy includes grief; the loss of self-esteem manifests as self-reproach.

Emotional loss is translated as the abandonment of maternal attachment, the first process of substitution, arising from the physiological and emotional recognition of the mother through inheritance. It is the mother who initiates the first resolution of loss.

From a psychological perspective, it refers to the process a human being undergoes in the face of the irreversible loss of memory, reason, or emotionality. For this reason, if feelings are avoided or evaded in an attempt to mitigate pain, the grieving process can be delayed or prolonged.

When reason takes over all emotions and, consequently, sensations, it reaches a psychological extension where the imagination plays a very painful role, and it cannot be eliminated without paying the price of simulation or fantasy.

Death is not the greatest loss, but rather what dies inside the individual.

Experiencing loss and witnessing it stirs emotions and confronts us with unpleasant sensations, such as the helplessness to alleviate pain and suffering. Knowing that the only true comfort would be the return of the person.

Depending on the degree of attachment and separation, sadness and pain may persist for a longer time.

The emotional, cognitive, social, familial, occupational, spiritual, and cultural process redefines goals and objectives, emphasizing the reconstruction of the individual within their life context.

Giving Meaning to Life in the Face of Losses

It is not unusual for someone who has suffered a loss to wish for death, either to relieve the unbearable pain they feel or to reunite with the deceased person in a better world.

One loses themselves in the other, to the point of losing the role they had in that person's presence. For example, a woman becomes a widow and what she loses is the security her spouse provided.

It is the absence of the "self" that existed for the other. When a mother loses her only child, she also loses her sense of motherhood. When someone loses their job, they lose the ability to practice their profession. When a woman loses a breast, she loses what that part of her body symbolized, nurturing capacity, motherhood, sensual expression, etc.

In losses, symbolic aspects are also lost. For example, losing a job not only results in the loss of income, but also the economy, status, and power that came with the position. The individual experiences a loss of meaning and thus loses the ability to socialize, connect, or interact with the outside world.

Bowlby, in a study on unprocessed grief related to Charles Darwin's childhood, found that unresolved grief correlated with frequent physical ailments (gastrointestinal problems, fatigue, palpitations, etc.) and psychological issues (depression, anxiety, low self-esteem) that plagued him throughout most of his life.

The need to process grief and loss requires addressing feelings of sadness, desolation, longing, nostalgia, and anxiety.

The importance of giving new meaning to the loss is understanding that you do not lose what has been gained; you only lose what is lost. Sooner or later, adaptation forces one to let go of the prolonged suffering caused by absence.

On one hand, there is a sense of fulfillment from having shared experiences, and on the other, releasing emotions tied to the narrative or the symbolic, which makes behavior more adaptable to new life conditions.

The profound emptiness felt from living a superficial life, devoid of commitments, is what causes attachments to other people in an attempt to mitigate the pain of their inevitable loss.

Every change implies a loss, and any loss is impossible without change.

Reflecting on the loss and reviewing memories are ways to take a break from the intense anguish that accompanies the active process of grief.

Loss tends to establish a process that fluctuates between feeling and doing.

Missing

It is common to find that much of the chronic nature of grief is due to the unresolved management of the absence of the self in the other self. In other words, what is missed most is what the person represented, rather than the actual loss itself. One may feel the afflictions of sadness and guilt.

After feeling unprotected by the shock, and once anger and avoidance have been externalized, one experiences loneliness and sadness in their full intensity.

It is necessary to maintain this difficult balance between remembering the past and investing in the future while feeling the absence for the rest of one's life.

The adaptation in the first two years following a death or significant loss, as a way to normalize the experience, allows for a more realistic anticipation of its duration.

Making Sense of Life in the Face of Loss

An emotional detachment is needed, one that can mark continuity and resurgence in the here and now.

It is not uncommon for an individual who has suffered a loss to wish for death, either to relieve the unbearable pain they feel or to reunite with the departed person in a better world.

Attachment

According to Bowlby, emotional loss is a way of conceptualizing the predisposition to form strong bonds that manifest as emotional pain and personality disorders such as anxiety, anger, depression, and emotional detachment, which result from unwanted separation. There is a need to bond, and therefore distress is seen as a reaction to the threat of loss. This often occurs when one feels ignored or rejected.

It is difficult to let go of those we love, and it hurts to feel no longer loved. One begins to experience the emptiness that causes despair; however, in that process, there is progress toward growth and maturation. If one manages to assimilate the act of letting go, a part of their own history will be left behind, and new feelings, often accompanied by fear of the unknown and something different, will arise.

The serious conflict that arises if one does not learn to let go, to unhook, and to release what has been lost, what is longed for, and what has become a need at some point, will result in painful attachment to dreams, fantasies, expectations, and illusions. The pain will grow day by day, and suddenly, without realizing it, joy will fade away, making room for sadness and suffering to enter without mercy. These will become companions along the journey, leading to apathy, desolation, lack of motivation, feelings of depression, and a loss of meaning in life.

Reframing Losses

Attachments/Detachments
Memories... belong to time
Material things... belong to the earth
Partners, children, significant others... belong to the heart
Friends and family... belong to the journey
Body... property of the earth
Soul... belongs to God (the universe), belief system
Talents from circumstances
Empty suitcase... when we die, the moments are taken, everything else stays behind

Chapter 6
Promoting Autonomy

Stress Reduction

Stress derives from the Latin word *stringere*, which means "to provoke tension." The word was first used around the 14th century.

Stress is the way the brain and body react. They respond to any interpretation they are given and perceive. It can manifest in the face of any kind of challenge, change, or traumatic event, including losses and even death itself, affecting one's health.

Events in the surrounding environment can alter and disorganize the body. It is essential to maintain personal adjustment to changes in order to achieve stability in one's internal environment. Otherwise, the disruption of balance in the body can lead to stress.

According to the French philosopher Claudie Bernard (1867), stress results in somatic and psychological consequences, which manifest as symptoms that can be divided into three categories:

Physical symptoms: such as tachycardia, sweating, body tremors, cold hands and feet, muscle tension, loss or increase of appetite, diarrhea or constipation, insomnia, stuttering, fatigue, dry mouth, etc.

Psychological symptoms: such as a desire to cry, difficulty concentrating, decreased memory, anxiety, excessive worry, thinking of terrifying scenes, catastrophic thinking, slow thinking, irritability, and constant mood swings, etc.

Behavioral symptoms: such as nervous laughter, constant movement, the urge to run and hide, grinding of teeth, among others. If these symptoms are not recognized and addressed in time, they can trigger or worsen illnesses like colds, gastritis, colitis, ulcers, migraines, muscle contractures, arthritis, high blood pressure, allergies, asthma, diabetes mellitus, heart attacks, and cancer, among others.

Emotions trigger responses in motor, cognitive, and physiological aspects. They are basic mechanisms of the human condition and play a role in adaptive functions, such as anxiety, fear, sadness, guilt, or joy, to name a few.

In the motor aspect: avoidance and escape behaviors, compulsive and impulsive behaviors, and motor disability.

In the cognitive aspect: physiological, behavioral, and emotional reactions can be modified, such as: worries, demoralization, apprehension, thought confusion, difficulties with attention and concentration.

In the physiological aspect: high activation of the autonomic nervous system, which brings a series of physiological changes such as tachycardia, dizziness, sweating, blushing, stomach tension, or respiratory difficulties.

Cognitive factors related to the interpretation of events play a very important role in determining what is stressful. The rigidity of stress occurs when the significance and quality of the goals being threatened are prolonged over an extended period of time.

Events such as the death of a loved one are universally stressful stimuli. For an event to be considered stressful, it must be perceived as a threat, and one must lack the resources to cope with it effectively, as Folkman (1986) mentions. As a result, the same event may be stressful at times, but at other times may not produce any stress reaction.

The general adaptation syndrome is useful for explaining people's responses to stress, but it is not specific in interpreting which stimuli cause stress for a particular person. It is important to reflect on the connections between the past and the present, which influence how one selects, interprets, and reacts to interpersonal events. Ignoring these connections may lead to post-traumatic stress disorder (PTSD), which involves the repeated, distressing re-experiencing of trauma, making it necessary to seek professional help.

Taking time to feel and reflect on one's current state and assessing one's capacities to modify or change and take responsibility for one's health is essential.

Distress and Anxiety

These are two terms related to a feeling of danger in the face of something undefined.

The word *distress* comes from the root "ang," meaning "to tighten."

Anxiety, etymologically, means "discomfort" and consists of an undefined fear, whose function, under normal conditions, is to alert the body to the presence of danger, stimulating the individual's response capacity.

According to Freud in 1926, normal anxiety is distinguished by its relation to a known danger, while pathological or neurotic anxiety is a danger that must be discovered.

Anxiety can manifest physically or bodily through fatigue, irritability, poor concentration, muscle tension, hyperactivity (palpitations), sweating, pain, diarrhea, stomach aches, dry mouth, increased urination, sleep disorders, etc.

The term anxiety is used to describe psychological symptoms experienced as restlessness and sudden alarm.

The difference between distress and anxiety is determined by the intensity of the manifestations.

According to Dr. Teresa Robles, it is distinguished in three different areas:

Behavioral: in actions.
Cognitive: in thoughts.
Physiological: in physiological or biological reactions.

Panic disorder is defined by a spontaneous episode of intense anxiety. It can lead to the abuse of alcohol and tranquilizers.

Fear may resemble anxiety; it is used when the anxious feeling arises in response to a specific external stimulus that the individual perceives as a danger or threat.

Distress is not directed at something specific; it is an undefined sensation, lacking an object. The anticipation of real fear is the basis of distress.

Authors such as Rank, Goldstein, and May consider anxiety to be normal, intrinsic to the process of individualization, and a result of personal development and evolution.

Pathological anxiety is characterized by tension, discomfort, unease, and undefined fear, which affects daily activities. The individual experiences reduced personal freedom, and anxiety becomes a disproportionate emotion, even appearing in the absence of any manifest danger.

Pathological anxiety is considered when the intensity, proportion, and duration of the organism's activation state exceed normal limits.

According to Henry Ey, the pathology of anxiety is characterized as being **"Anachronic"**: the individual relives past situations.

Phantasmagoric: an imaginary representation of an unconscious conflict.

Stereotyped: it is repetitive.

Pathological anxiety is more physical and, at its extreme, manifests as distress, persisting beyond adaptive limits, affecting performance and psychosocial functioning. Sheehan classifies anxiety in connection with the environment:

Exogenous anxiety: arises from personal or psychosocial external stimuli, related to stress, and includes spontaneous panic attacks.

Endogenous anxiety: this is an autonomous sensation, relatively independent of environmental stimuli and linked to genetic vulnerability. The response to pharmacological therapy is good. It presents with symptoms of unexplained panic or anxiety attacks and is associated with multiple phobias. Pathological anxiety can be differentiated into state anxiety and trait anxiety.

State anxiety: includes panic attacks, distress states, and anxiety reactions.

Trait anxiety: a tendency to react anxiously, considered a personality variable.

According to Freud, anxiety disorders are the result of an intrapsychic conflict without an organic basis. This includes hysterical, phobic, and obsessive neuroses.

In his description of anxiety neurosis, Freud identifies ten characteristics, which we now call pathological anxiety: general irritability, apprehensive anticipation, floating anxiety, development of phobias, gastrointestinal disorders, paresthesias, and a tendency toward chronicity.

In panic attacks, there are three main elements: fear of going insane, fear of dying, or fear of losing control; the progression of the crisis to anticipatory anxiety, and avoidant behavior.

In 1977, the WHO replaced the term anxiety neurosis with anxious state.

In panic disorder and generalized anxiety disorder, avoidance is the characteristic behavior of panic disorder with agoraphobia.

In obsessive-compulsive disorder, the individual struggles against their obsessions or compulsions.

Anxiety and depression are the most common, with women being more prone to anxiety disorders. The most frequent age of onset is between 20 and 40 years. It is more common in lower socioeconomic levels. Patients with panic disorders often develop secondary depressive symptoms. Hypochondriasis is a consequence of generalized anxiety.

Generalized anxiety disorder consists of persistent and generalized feelings of anxiety, manifesting as chronic and sustained internal tension.

Anxiety does not appear in response to a specific stimulus and is unmotivated and disproportionate. There are excessive worries without any real justification. Symptoms include headaches, gastrointestinal issues, instability, dizziness, tingling, and sensations of heaviness and fatigue, along with irritability and insomnia. By contrast, panic attacks occur suddenly and are characterized by the intensity of anxiety symptoms. In generalized anxiety disorder, the symptoms are prolonged, persistent, and therefore of lesser intensity.

Panic attacks: episodes that appear suddenly without a known triggering factor, occurring both on the psychological and somatic levels. They can cause apprehension and fear, leaving the patient confused, fatigued, and exhausted.

The first episode is remembered very precisely, and it usually occurs when the person is calm, without any apparent reason to justify the attack. It limits work and social activities, leading to pathological dependence in order to always be accompanied, as this is the only way the person feels safe.

Somatic illness: patients with anxiety disorders somatize, developing conditions such as high blood pressure, peptic ulcers, and cardiovascular disease. Hyperthyroidism, whose symptoms can be mistaken for a panic attack.

Some of the symptoms that commonly appear during a panic attack due to stress include:

Shortness of breath or difficulty breathing
Palpitations
Chest pain or discomfort
Breathlessness or a sensation of choking
Dizziness, vertigo, or a feeling of instability
Feeling of unreality
Tingling in hands and feet
Hot and cold flashes
Sweating
Weakness
Trembling or shaking
Fear of dying, going insane, or losing control

	DISTRESS	**ANXIETY**	**FEAR**
Origin	Constriction	Discomfort/ Indeterminate	Real/Imaginary
Expressions	Physical	Psychic/Sense of threat	Psychic/Sense of threat
Sensations	Limitation	Restlessness/ Feeling of threat	Reason to take action
Reaction	Chest tightness Stomach discomfort Shortness of breath	Feeling of death Inability to escape	Escape/ Avoidance

Normal and Pathological Anxiety

	NORMAL	PATHOLOGICAL
Intensity	Mild	Deep, persistent
Relation to the environment	Compensated, activating	Disproportionate, hyperactivation
Manifestations	Psychic	Somatic
Objective	Enhances resources	Lacks a concrete objective
Duration	Related to the stimulus	Indeterminate, autonomous
Temporal origin	Current moment	Anachronic (past)
Consequences	Freedom, adaptation	Loss of freedom

Depression

Feelings of depression can be described as feeling sad, melancholic, unhappy, miserable, unmotivated, hopeless, abandoned, or broken down. Most people feel this way from time to time for short periods. Clinical depression is a mood disorder where feelings of sadness, loss, anger, or frustration interfere with daily life over a prolonged period. Physical causes that can show symptoms of depression must be ruled out before making a diagnosis.

Many researchers believe it may be caused by chemical imbalances in the brain, which may be hereditary or triggered by life events. Some episodes of depression cannot be prevented.

Low self-esteem is often associated with depression, as are sudden outbursts of anger and a lack of pleasure in activities that usually make the person happy, including sexual activity, which can trigger the onset of a depressive episode. Depression is more common in women than in men and is especially prevalent during the teenage years.

There are four personality traits that can increase the likelihood of developing depression: nervousness, a negative way of thinking, passive behavior patterns, and obsessive perfectionism.

Depression manifests when five or more symptoms of depression are present for at least two weeks. These include: melancholy, discouragement, sadness, disappointment, lack of motivation, mood changes, hopelessness, worthlessness, or pessimism. The use of the Beck Depression Inventory is also common.

Symptoms

- Difficulty falling asleep or excessive sleep
- Significant changes in appetite, often leading to weight gain or loss
- Fatigue and lack of energy
- Feelings of worthlessness, self-hatred, and inappropriate guilt
- Extreme difficulty concentrating
- Agitation, restlessness, and irritability
- Inactivity and withdrawal from usual activities; a loss of interest or pleasure in activities once enjoyed (such as sexual activity)
- Feelings of hopelessness and abandonment
- Thoughts of death or suicide

Recurrences can be prevented with treatments that include medication and psychiatric intervention.

It is important to maintain a healthy lifestyle that includes:

- Getting enough sleep
- Eating a nutritious and healthy diet
- Exercising regularly
- Avoiding alcohol, marijuana, and other psychoactive drugs
- Engaging in activities that usually bring happiness, even if there is no desire to do so
- Spending time with family and friends
- Considering prayer or meditation
- Trying to speak with clergy or spiritual counselors who can help make sense of painful experiences
- Seeking supportive interpersonal relationships

Common Causes

- The death of a family member, friend, or pet.
- A significant disappointment at home, work, or school with friends (such as a breakup, failing a subject, or parental divorce).
- Prolonged pain or serious illness.
- Medical conditions like hypothyroidism (low thyroid activity), cancer, or hepatitis.
- Medications such as tranquilizers and drugs for high blood pressure.
- Excessive alcohol or drug use.
- Chronic stress.
- Childhood events such as abuse or rejection.
- Social isolation (common in the elderly).
- Nutritional deficiencies (such as folate and omega-3 fatty acids).
- Sleep problems.

Depression is generally classified by severity: mild, moderate, or severe.

Severe depression: 5 or more symptoms from the list above must be present for at least two weeks, though this condition tends to persist for at least 6 months.

Depression is classified as minor or moderate if fewer than 5 symptoms are present for at least two weeks.

Severe depression can be accompanied by psychotic symptoms, such as hallucinations and delusions, which are usually consistent with the depressed mood and may focus on themes of guilt, personal inadequacy, or illness. It often involves behavioral changes, like altered sleep and eating patterns. This type of depression increases the risk of suicide.

Dysthymia: a chronic form of depression, generally milder, but lasts longer, often up to 2 years.

Atypical depression: depression accompanied by unusual symptoms, such as hallucinations (e.g., hearing voices that aren't really there) or delusions (irrational thoughts).

Other common forms of depression include:

Postpartum depression: many women feel depressed after giving birth, but it is uncommon.

Premenstrual dysphoric disorder (PMDD): depressive symptoms occur a week before menstruation and disappear after menstruation.

Seasonal affective disorder (SAD): occurs during the fall and winter months and disappears in the spring and summer, likely due to a lack of sunlight.

Depression can also occur with mania (known as manic depression or bipolar disorder). In this condition, moods cycle between mania and depression.

The person should seek medical assistance immediately if:

- They hear voices that aren't there.
- They experience frequent crying episodes, with or without provocation.
- They have had feelings of depression that disrupt work, school, or family life for more than two weeks.
- They exhibit 3 or more symptoms of depression.
- They think that one of the medications they are currently taking may be causing depression. However, medications SHOULD NOT be changed or discontinued without consulting a doctor first.
- They have ever had thoughts of ending their life.

"Pain is a great teacher when it sends us back to reality and, in turn, invites us to serve and help others."

Improving Quality of Life

The terms "quality of life" and "well-being" are used by doctors and psychologists; however, other terms exist in biology, described as "adaptive potential," or in psychological terms such as "efficacy" or "power." Another term is "standard of living." Sen (1992) refers to this variant of quality of life as "capability." An individual's capability will depend on whether they are prepared to face life's challenges. At other times, the term "health" is used in a medical context. Health and illness are the result of either success or failure to adapt physically, mentally, socially, and spiritually to the conditions of our environment.

The World Health Organization (WHO, 1964) defines health as "a state of complete physical, mental, and social well-being, and not merely the absence of disease or infirmity."

Illness occurs when a person becomes stuck, living permanently in the "now past" or in expectations derived from a "now future."

What is quality of life? It is a very personal sense of well-being and will depend on each individual, as it can be perceived both "objectively" and "subjectively." Objectivity refers to a standard of living that meets clear patterns of a good life, evaluated by an impartial external observer. For example, when talking about death, it is something natural that everyone will eventually face. Subjectivity, on the other hand, refers to self-assessments based on manifest reasoning, for example, when talking about death as an indescribable, heartbreaking pain that one wishes to avoid.

If the environment is favorable and there is a positive subjective appreciation, it can be defined as "well-being." For example: objectively, the afternoon is sunny, and subjectively, it is said to be the best weather for swimming.

When a person accepts their own feelings, they integrate with others, balance out, and everything becomes harmonious.

Factors Related to Well-Being and Quality of Life:

- Stopping self-blame and the "shoulds" helps to avoid self-punishment.
- Stop creating expectations for others to make you feel good.
- Develop faith and confidence in oneself.
- As one stops trying to please others, self-respect and self-value increase.

Pérez Farfán (2007) suggests that before applying knowledge to serve others, it is essential to apply it to ourselves. Scientifically, there is a known relationship between the immune system and neural pathways, and their direct interaction in the production of lymphocytes. Stress depresses the immune system, making us more vulnerable.

Adaptive Process

Personality traits are persistent patterns of relating to and thinking about the environment and oneself, which are manifested in a wide range of social and personal contexts.

Personality traits only constitute personality disorders when they are inflexible and maladaptive, causing significant functional impairment or subjective distress. They affect the cognitive, affective, interpersonal, or impulse control areas. Personal qualities such as a sense of humor, courage, perseverance, self-awareness, a spirit of adventure, etc., result in resilience, where one's ability adapts to the process of situational change.

Unfortunately, traumatic experiences and situations of loss will represent a difficult process of adaptation. It is important to gradually accept the undesirable consequences of such events.

When talking about severe stress and adjustment disorders, the best coping resources are tested. As a holistic human being, one interacts with culture, which influences them, adopting values, knowledge, beliefs, and attitudes, while seeking virtues or stability to process loss.

Malleability does not deform; it reforms. It does not destroy; it builds. This is the goal of Thanatodynamics: to drive adaptation, to adjust, to become one with the surroundings. And after becoming, to accept the transformation that transcends and never perishes.

It is important to take personal control, moving from worry to action in the search for resilience. Recognizing and accepting that in the process of grief and loss one cannot manage alone will help reflect on the need to seek help from a professional, because pretending it doesn't hurt… hurts twice as much.

Intervention:

Thanatologist – Loss and hopelessness (inject hope and transcendence)

Psychologist – Active listening

Doctor – Heals the body

You get sick… you heal yourself.

In grief, death (loss) takes the soul.

It will help to ask oneself:

To care for my mind, thoughts, anxiety, and stress levels, what am I doing that makes me feel bad? (Isolation, overuse of social media and alarming news, thinking I can get through it without therapeutic support).

What do I feel, and how do I feel about what causes me stress/fear/anger/sadness/rage/pain/grief? Why do I feel this way?

Of the things that worry me, which can I change?

What will my attitude be toward the things I cannot change?

Regarding perception, what will I do differently to take responsibility for improving my physical health? (Maintaining a healthy weight, exercising, eating well, having regular medical check-ups, seeking happy moments).

Feeling like a victim, blaming others, or blaming oneself drains energy, vitality, and ultimately leads to emotional and physical exhaustion. It's a way of surrendering power to external forces, including unresolved tasks that are postponed. This makes one feel uncomfortable, losing energy, concentration, and intention to do truly meaningful things, leading to frustration. This frustration feeds thoughts that damage one's self-perception, causing emotional symptoms that will eventually trigger physical symptoms.

Chapter 7
Resources for Coping with Grief and Loss

It is vital to identify mental fatigue, as it is a mix of lack of interest and physical exhaustion that causes symptoms. It is each person's responsibility to give their brain, nerves, and muscles a break; there are techniques, dynamics, and exercises to help with this.

Test to Understand Your Attitude Toward Grief or Loss

How would you define what you are feeling?

How has it affected your life?

How have your feelings changed up until now?

What does grief mean to you?

Can you describe your interpretation of your loss?

How does your loss make you feel?

Can you describe how you reacted to your loss?

Have you noticed any changes in your self-perception?

Did your religious or spiritual beliefs help you cope with the loss?

Of all your losses, which do you think is the most significant?

How did you express your grief or loss?

Did you feel supported at the time of your loss?

Do you feel you have learned anything from your loss?

Could there be any benefit from that loss?

How does the reaction of others make you feel?

Do others understand what you need?

Do others have the willingness and the means to meet your needs?

What does this represent for you and for everyone else?

Would you like to start reinterpreting what you've lost?

Dynamic

Suggested Tasks for Reorganizing the System After Loss

Recognize emotions to infer needs and channel them in the best way possible.

Identify needs to establish assertive communication, enabling one to listen and speak without feeling judged.

Observe the effect of emotions and thoughts on physical well-being.

Breathe: don't let the pain steal the air from your chest. Allow the body to oxygenate.

If the nature of the pain is due to illness, identifying its source may stem from perceptions and interpretations, which could block treatment. It is important to recognize the type of ailment the body is suffering and acknowledge it. Do not resist the pain, because what you resist persists, and as a consequence, it will impact psychological pain projected onto the physical body.

Supportive Exercises

Physical: Healthy, mindful eating, physical and breathing exercises.

Emotional: Conscious relationships, breathing exercises, relaxation, visualization.

Mental: Reflection, mindful attention, updating abilities.

Spiritual: Working on expanding consciousness and "being present"; meditation helps.

Conscious Breathing: It is the gateway to relaxation, allowing deep breathing to access areas of the mind and observe what is happening.

Relaxation: Its benefits are observed both on a physiological and psychological or spiritual level.

It is a source of vitality, fostering an attitude of inner peace, balance, and equanimity.

Hypnotherapy and Imagery

Techniques

Relaxation Techniques

Techniques to modify behavior against tension, anxiety, or depression acquired from unpleasant situations such as grief or loss.

These techniques modify the physiological components of tension, such as breathing rate, pulse rate, and muscle contraction.

They are based on a physiological approach, especially for people who do not respond well to perception and can help reduce medication usage.

Benson's Techniques are simple:

The environment should be calm and preferably dark.

Sit upright on a comfortable chair with your hands resting on your thighs, palms down.

Breathe slowly, deeply, and deliberately. Focus on the experience of exhaling. While doing this, repeat any chosen monosyllabic word. Benson prefers the word "one."

Adopt a passive attitude. If the mind wanders, accept that it may return, and refocus on observing the breath and concentrating on exhalation.

Breathing Dynamic – 3 times

With the great power of the mind, imagine how the breath travels through the body: head, nose, ears, eyes, neck, heart, organs, stomach, legs, hands, and fingers.

Rest: Let go of worries and release tension.

Rest for 5 to 10 minutes, especially after digestion.

Stress: Releasing Anger

The responsibility for emotions depends on the meaning given to the working hours.

It is necessary to take a break between two different activities.

The body needs 7 to 8 hours of rest daily. :Sleeping is not the same as resting.

The morning hours are the most advisable for activities that require concentration.

What is the technique for sleeping? Lie down in bed, close your eyes, breathe deeply, and exhale slowly several times.

What Factors Influence Mental Fatigue?

Environment (light, sound, temperature).

Mood.

Lack of interest, food.

Faith is the confidence that what we hope for will actually happen; it gives us assurance about things we cannot see (Hebrews 11:1).

An idea generates thinking, feeling, and acting.

Responding is learning to see, hear, and feel oneself.

Focus on gains (what you still have) and stop looking at what you no longer have.

Find a "happy hour" every day.

Exercise to Help Identify Feelings, Thoughts, and Actions

Ask yourself:

What do I feel?

Is my sleep restorative, and how many hours do I sleep?

If I have insomnia, how often?

Do I struggle with concentration, memory loss, or effort to recall and relax?

When thinking, do recurring memories of the loved one appear, thoughts of terrifying scenes, destructive or catastrophic thoughts, a feeling of strangeness, disbelief, general disinterest in daily activities, slow thinking, confusion, or worry?

Have I had recurring thoughts of seeing life without interest, to the point of losing the will to live?

Regarding behavior, are there sleep disturbances, such as oversleeping or difficulty sleeping, insomnia, dreaming about the loss or the loved one, nervous laughter, crying, avoiding memories, moving unusually or constantly, seeking objects or anything related to the loved one and treasuring them, the need to run and hide, or teeth grinding?

Speaking of emotions, is there guilt, instability, anger, suppressed rage, fatigue, emotional exhaustion, helplessness, constant crying, self-blame, grief, frequent mental blocks, desolation, anxiety, constant mood swings, sadness, longing, powerlessness, and frustration?

The importance of allowing oneself to feel physically is vital for properly channeling the emotions and sensations caused by unpleasant symptoms.

It is necessary to ask: Do I feel tachycardia, frequent headaches, chest pain, constant sighing, dry mouth, sweating, shortness of breath, body tremors, cold hands and feet, loss or increase of appetite, an empty feeling in the stomach, diarrhea or constipation, stuttering, lack of energy, fatigue, chest or throat tightness, muscle tension or weakness to the point of stabbing or burning pains, hypersensitivity to noise?

Describing your day-to-day experiences helps to stay in touch with yourself and identify if new symptoms appear that weren't present before, allowing you to address them and avoid getting sick.

Tips

It doesn't matter how one chooses to grieve. There is no "right" way to do it.

Grief is a normal emotion, and it will fade.

Express and release emotions—scream, cry, hit things. It's better not to repress them. If, occasionally, you see or hear something that reminds you of the person who is gone or of the object, it's necessary to connect with those memories to help process the loss.

Express yourself freely, perhaps in writing, starting with how you feel and what it means.

Don't feel pressured to talk (I once met someone who lost their voice); it was the time to feel, not to speak.

If people say, "Don't cry, you're not letting them rest"… and you hold back, the pain gets trapped and doesn't leave.

Participate in rituals. Religious services help overcome the loss and honor the deceased.

Gathering with others gives a sense of support and helps prevent isolation (such as rosary groups).

Exercise helps as an "emotional pill" (oxytocin, dopamine, serotonin, and endorphins); it can change bad moods and pessimism. Modify your routine if necessary.

Eat well—the body needs nutritious food, drink water, and avoid dehydration.

Do "BRAIN GYM" exercises.

Rest is not just about sleeping (help your mind by doing the alphabet in reverse).

Join support groups—remember, it's not necessary to be alone with feelings of grief.

Change that negative memory into something positive by reinterpreting the loss and finding gain.

Recognizing and trying to live through the pain is an expression of mental health.

A good therapist doesn't tell you what to do—they provide dynamics, and the affected person acts.

NOTE... If grief has turned into depression and it has lasted more than three months without being able to continue with regular activities, or if thoughts of suicide, death, or self-harm arise… it is necessary to seek professional help.

EPILOGUE

Culture is the path through which we express our human condition, and the grieving process is the gateway to understanding that pain and loneliness. The individual task is to find personal resources that help with self-identification. The challenge lies in becoming emotionally independent, as most of the time, we are affected by the desires, needs, or shortcomings of others. Learning the gains despite the losses helps us assimilate and recognize our own. Belonging to oneself from a place of solitude, accepting that functionality comes from deep respect for one's individuality. Loving oneself is not an easy task; accepting the story of pain is necessary to heal the wounds and live with autonomy and freedom. Otherwise, we are condemned to hurt others.

Therefore, maintaining, transforming, and reinterpreting the experience that pain left behind means living consciously, acknowledging that we continue to be nourished by what comes from the past, constantly creating the present, and opening the future.

Undoubtedly, by opening the heart and mind, one can avoid needing a health specialist, because when you are healthy, you don't require someone to "heal" you.

To know how my body will feel today, it is enough to remember what I thought, felt, and did yesterday.

Illness comes from within, so it is each person's responsibility to stay well. "I get sick, I heal myself."

Life is meant to be lived today; there is no "later." This book is an invitation not to lose oneself in pain.

GLOSSARY

Affliction: Represents the particular subjective reactions experienced while living in a state of grief (what one feels, the pain of sorrow). This is where we find the greatest differences.

Anguish: A state of great emotional arousal containing a feeling of fear or apprehension. Clinically defined as a fear reaction to an unclear and unknown danger. It is also used as a synonym for anxiety or to refer to its most extreme expression.

Anxiety: Anticipatory fear of future harm or misfortune, accompanied by a feeling of dread or somatic symptoms of tension.

Apathy: Emotional numbness. A state in which the individual remains indifferent.

Learning: A permanent change in a person's behavior as a result of experience. It refers to the change in behavior or potential behavior of a subject in a given situation, as a result of repeated experiences in that situation. This behavioral change cannot be explained by the individual's innate response tendencies, maturation, or temporary states (such as fatigue, alcohol intoxication, impulses, etc.).

Aptitude: The ability to benefit from any teaching, training, or experience in a given area of performance.

Association: A mental process by which one idea is spontaneously linked to another.

Aspiration: A goal the individual sets for themselves when completing a specific task.

Attention: The ability to focus persistently on a specific stimulus or activity.

Capabilities: Hypothetical mental aptitudes that allow the human mind to act and perceive.

Character: A set of traits that distinguish one person from another.

Character, neurosis of: Exaggeration of certain personality traits, leading to behavioral disorders.

Cognition: Conscious processing of thoughts and images.

Compensation: An unconscious psychological mechanism by which an individual tries to counteract real or imagined inferiority.

Consciousness: A structure of personality in which psychic phenomena are fully perceived and understood by the person.

Behavior: The overall reaction of an individual to different environmental situations.

Conflict: Two opposing motivations of equal intensity.

Panic attack: The sudden onset of anxiety at its maximum intensity. These attacks are experienced by the patient as a signal of imminent death; the intensity of the suffering is equivalent to that of someone who feels they are about to be killed. Accompanied by bodily symptoms of panic: tachycardia, palpitations, rapid breathing, a feeling of suffocation or shortness of breath, nausea or abdominal discomfort, dizziness, fainting, or disorientation, paleness, cold hands and feet, a sensation of precordial tightness, which can sometimes become chest pain, sweating, paresthesias (numbness or tingling), fear of losing control or "going crazy," and fear of dying.

Guilt, feeling of: A painful experience derived from a more or less conscious sense of having violated personal or social ethical norms.

Emotion: An affective state, a subjective reaction to the environment, accompanied by organic changes (physiological and endocrine) of innate origin, influenced by experience, and with an adaptive function. Emotions refer to internal states like desire or need, which direct the organism. Basic categories of emotions include fear, surprise, aversion, anger, sadness, and joy.

Empathy: A mental state in which an individual identifies with another group or person, sharing the same emotional state.

Mood: A generalized and persistent emotion that influences the perception of the world. Common examples of mood include depression, joy, anger, and anxiety.

Stimulant: A drug that increases an individual's motor and psychic activity.

Stimulus-response: A theory that explains how an individual's behavior consists of a set of reactions to preceding stimuli.

Stress: Any demand that produces a state of tension in an individual, requiring change or adaptation.

Psychosomatic illness: Illness caused or aggravated by psychological factors such as stress, lifestyle changes, personality variables, and emotional conflicts.

Irritable: Easily angered and prone to rage.

Hormones: Chemical substances produced in an organ and transported by the blood to cells in the body, exerting a regulatory physiological effect.

Feeling: Subjective description.

Somatic: Pertaining to or relating to the body's tissues.

Therapy: Treatment through activities to heal diseases, symptoms, thoughts, or dysfunction, and to solve psychological problems in order to reduce suffering.

www.ingramcontent.com/pod-product-compliance
Lightning Source LLC
LaVergne TN
LVHW051217070526
838200LV00063B/4935